Berries & blooms

These patchwork-and-appliqué quilts and pillows are a striking blend of modern color and pastoral elegance. Jan Kornfeind has embellished several designs in this collection with buttons, adding to their charm. Once you get started with your favorite quilt, don't be surprised if you find yourself hurrying to finish the entire collection of five wall hangings, three pillows, and the "berry" appealing table runner!

Meet jan kornfeind

Jan Kornfeind has always loved to sew. The former grade school teacher began making sample quilts for local quilt shops in order to be a stay-at-home mom with her son, Benjamin. As her work became popular, she realized her art could become her career. Jan began designing patterns in 1980, and thus evolved the company: Country Appliqués.

Her craftsmanship and love of color and folk art are the basis for selecting the subject matter of her designs. Jan says, "I love to design a picture and then find just the right fabrics and embellishments. That's sometimes a challenge, but always worth the effort to find the fabrics and colors that work best together."

Jan resides in Leawood, Kansas. You can find more of her captivating designs at www.countryappliques.com. And you are cordially invited to visit www.leisurearts.com or your local retailer to see Jan's first two Leisure Arts publications: #3827 Nature's Elegance and #3930 Quilted Furry Friends.

LEISURE ARTS, INC.
Little Rock, Arkansas

In Full Bloom *wall hanging*

Wall hanging assembled by Rosie Grinstead.
Finished Block Size: 8" x 8" (20 cm x 20 cm)
Finished Wall Hanging Size: 31" x 31" (79 cm x 79 cm)

YARDAGE REQUIREMENTS

Yardage is based on 43"/44" (109/112 cm) wide fabric.

- 3/8 yd (34 cm) **each** of 2 assorted cream print fabrics for backgrounds
- 1/4 yd (23 cm) of gold print fabric for sashing strips
- 1/8 yd (11 cm) of red/white check fabric for sashing squares
- 5/8 yd (57 cm) of red print fabric for borders
- 1 yd (91 cm) of fabric for backing
- 3/8 yd (34 cm) of fabric for binding
- Scraps of assorted green, red, gold, and black print fabrics for appliqués

You will also need:

- 35" x 35" (89 cm x 89 cm) piece of batting
- Paper-backed fusible web
- Stabilizer
- Buttons:
  - six 1/4" (7 mm) red round
  - nine 3/8" (9 mm) black round
  - 1/2" (13 mm) black round
  - 1/2" (13 mm) yellow star
  - 5/8" (16 mm) gold round

CUTTING OUT THE PIECES

*Follow **Rotary Cutting**, page 35, to cut fabric. All measurements include 1/4" seam allowances. Measurements for background squares include an extra 2". Trim to correct size after appliquéing. Cutting lengths for borders are exact. You may wish to add an extra 2" to length for "insurance," trimming borders to fit wall hanging top center.*

From each of 2 assorted cream print fabrics:
- Cut 2 **background squares** 10 1/2" x 10 1/2".

From gold print fabric:
- Cut 3 strips 2 1/2" wide. From these strips, cut 12 **sashing strips** 2 1/2" x 8 1/2".

From red/white check fabric:
- Cut 9 **sashing squares** 2 1/2" x 2 1/2".

From red print fabric:
- Cut 2 **top/bottom borders** 4 1/2" x 22 1/2".
- Cut 2 **side borders** 4 1/2" x 30 1/2".

From binding fabric:
- Cut 4 **binding strips** 2 1/2" wide.

CUTTING OUT THE APPLIQUÉS

*Follow **Preparing Fusible Appliqué Pieces**, page 36, to cut appliqués. Appliqué patterns, pages 8-11, do not include seam allowances and are reversed.*

Hibiscus

From scraps of assorted green print fabrics:
- Cut 1 **stem** (A).
- Cut 1 each of **leaves** (B and C).

From assorted red print fabrics:
- Cut 1 each of **hibiscus petals** (D – H).

From assorted gold print fabrics:
- Cut 1 **hibiscus inside petal** (I).
- Cut 2 **hibiscus inside petals** (J).
- Cut 1 **hibiscus inside petal** (K); cut 1 in reverse.

From black print fabric:
- Cut 1 **hibiscus center** (L).

Daisy

From assorted green print fabrics:
- Cut 1 **stem** (M).
- Cut 2 **leaves** (N).

From assorted gold print fabrics:
- Cut 4 each of **daisy petals** (O and P).

From black print fabric:
- Cut 1 **daisy large center** (Q).

From red print fabric:
- Cut 1 **daisy small center** (R).

Primrose

From assorted green print fabrics:
- Cut 1 **stem** (S).
- Cut 1 each of **leaves** (T and U).

From assorted gold print fabrics:
- Cut 1 each of **primrose petals** (V - Z).
- Cut 1 **primrose center** (DD).

From red print fabric:
- Cut 2 **primrose inside petals** (AA).
- Cut 3 **primrose inside petals** (BB).

From black print fabric:
- Cut 1 **primrose star center** (CC).

Poppy

From assorted green print fabrics:
- Cut 1 **stem** (EE).
- Cut 1 each of **leaves** (FF and GG).

From red print fabric:
- Cut 1 each of **poppy petals** (HH – LL).
- Cut 1 **poppy small center** (OO).

From black print fabric:
- Cut 1 **poppy large center** (MM).

From assorted gold print fabrics:
- Cut 1 **poppy medium center** (NN).

MAKING THE BLOCKS

Refer to block photos for placement.

1. Center and fuse appliqués for each flower to **background squares**.
2. Follow **Satin Stitch Appliqué**, page 36, to secure appliqués in place.
3. Centering the flowers within the block, trim background squares to 8½" x 8½".

ASSEMBLING THE WALL HANGING

*Follow **Machine Piecing** and **Pressing**, page 36, to make the blocks. Use a ¼" seam allowance for all seams. Refer to **Wall Hanging Diagram** for placement.*

1. Sew **Hibiscus Block**, **Daisy Block**, and 3 **sashing strips** together to make **Row 1**.
2. Sew **Primrose Block**, **Poppy Block**, and 3 **sashing strips** together to make **Row 2**.
3. Sew 3 **sashing squares** and 2 **sashing strips** together to make **Sashing Row**. Make 3 Sashing Rows.
4. Sew **Row 1**, **Row 2**, and **Sashing Rows** together to make **Wall Hanging Top Center**.
5. Matching centers and corners; sew **top/bottom borders** to **wall hanging top center**. Sew **side borders** to **wall hanging top center** to complete wall hanging top.

COMPLETING THE WALL HANGING

1. Follow **Quilting**, page 38, to mark, layer, and quilt as desired. Our wall hanging is machine quilted in the ditch around the sashing strips, sashing squares, and outside borders. It is echo quilted around the flowers, stems, and leaves. A cable design is quilted in the sashing strips and borders.
2. Follow **Making A Hanging Sleeve**, page 39, to make and attach a hanging sleeve, if desired.
3. Use binding strips and follow **Making Straight-Grain Binding**, page 40, to prepare binding.
4. Follow **Attaching Binding With Mitered Corners**, page 41, to attach binding to wall hanging.
5. Sew buttons to wall hanging in centers of flowers and sashing squares.

Hibiscus

Daisy

4

Wall Hanging Diagram

Primrose

Poppy

in full bloom *pillows*

Finished Pillow Size: 11" x 11" (28 cm x 28 cm)

YARDAGE REQUIREMENTS

Yardage is based on 43"/44" (109/112 cm) wide fabric and is for making 1 pillow.

Scraps of assorted gold, red, green, and black print fabrics for appliqués

1/2 yd (46 cm) of gold plaid fabric for pillow top and back

1/2 yd (46 cm) of red solid fabric for welting

3/8 yd (34 cm) of lining fabric

You will also need:

1 1/2 yds (1.4 m) of 1/4" (7 mm) diameter cord for welting

Polyester fiberfill

Paper-backed fusible web

Stabilizer

Desired buttons — We used one 1/4" (7 mm) gold round and one 1/2" (13 mm) red round on the Hibiscus pillow and one 1/2" (13 mm) gold star button on the Poppy pillow.

CUTTING OUT THE PIECES

Follow **Rotary Cutting**, *page 35, to cut fabric. Follow* **Making A Continuous Bias Strip**, *page 40, to cut bias strip. All measurements include* 1/4" *seam allowances.*

From gold plaid fabric:
- Cut 1 **pillow front** 13¹/₂" x 13¹/₂".
- Cut 1 **pillow back** 11¹/₂" x 11¹/₂".

From red solid fabric:
- Cut 1 **bias strip** 2" x 56", pieced as necessary.

From lining fabric:
- Cut 2 **lining squares** 11¹/₂" x 11¹/₂".

CUTTING OUT THE APPLIQUÉS

Follow **Preparing Fusible Appliqué Pieces**, *page 36, to cut appliqués. We used the Hibiscus and Poppy patterns, pages 8-9 and 11.* **Note:** *If you are using a different flower, refer to* **In Full Bloom Wall Hanging**, *Cutting Out The Appliqués, page 3, to cut appliqués for desired flower. Appliqué patterns do not include seam allowances and are reversed.*

Hibiscus

From assorted green print fabrics:
- Cut 1 **stem** (A).
- Cut 1 of each **leaf** (B and C).

From assorted red print fabrics:
- Cut 1 each of **hibiscus petals** (D) – (H).

From assorted gold print fabrics:
- Cut 1 **hibiscus inside petal** (I).
- Cut 2 **hibiscus inside petals** (J).
- Cut 1 **hibiscus inside petals** (K); cut 1 in reverse.

From black print fabric:
- Cut 1 **hibiscus center** (L).

Poppy

From assorted green print fabrics:
- Cut 1 **stem** (EE).
- Cut 1 of each **leaf** (FF and GG).

From assorted red print fabric:
- Cut 1 each of **poppy petals** (HH) – (LL).
- Cut 2 **poppy small center** (OO).

From black print fabric:
- Cut 1 **poppy large center** (MM).

From gold print fabric:
- Cut 1 **poppy medium center** (NN).

MAKING THE PILLOW

Use a 1/4" *seam allowance for all seams. Refer to* **Pillow Top Diagrams** *for placement.*

1. Center and fuse desired appliqués to **pillow front**.
2. Follow **Satin Stitch Appliqué**, page 36, to secure appliqués in place.
3. Centering the flower within the square, trim pillow front to 11¹/₂" x 11¹/₂".
4. Baste a **lining square** to wrong side of pillow front and pillow back.
5. Follow **Quilting**, page 38, to quilt pillow front as desired. Our pillow front is machine outline quilted around each flower, stem, and leaf.
6. Sew button(s) to center of flower as desired.
7. Follow **Pillow Finishing**, page 42, to add welting to pillow top and to finish pillow.

Hibiscus Pillow Top Diagram

Poppy Pillow Top Diagram

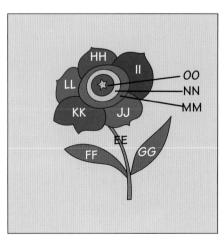

Hibiscus

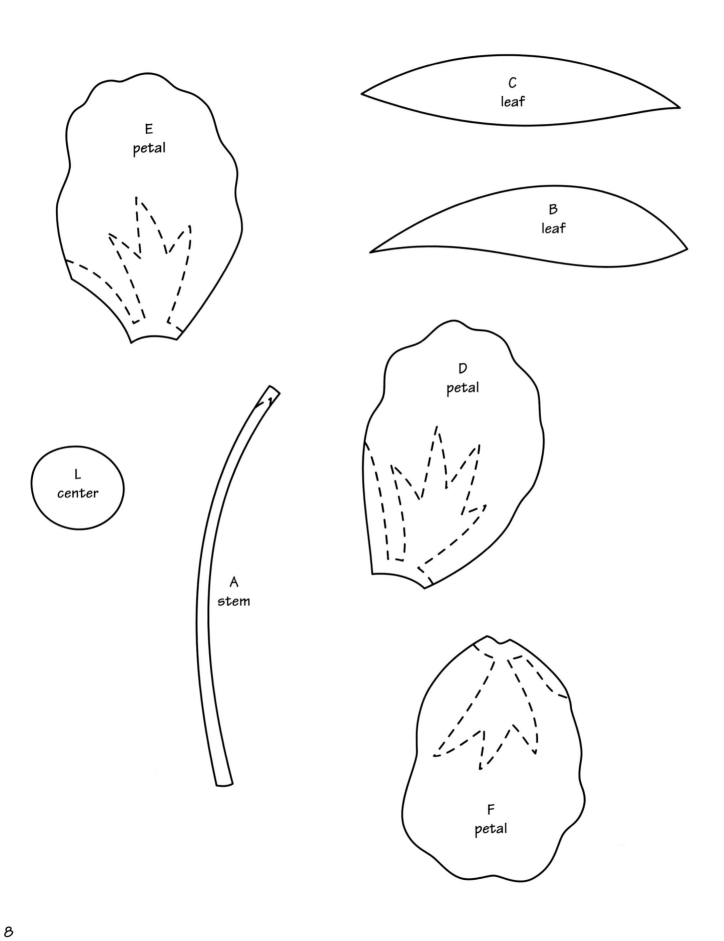

C
leaf

E
petal

B
leaf

D
petal

L
center

A
stem

F
petal

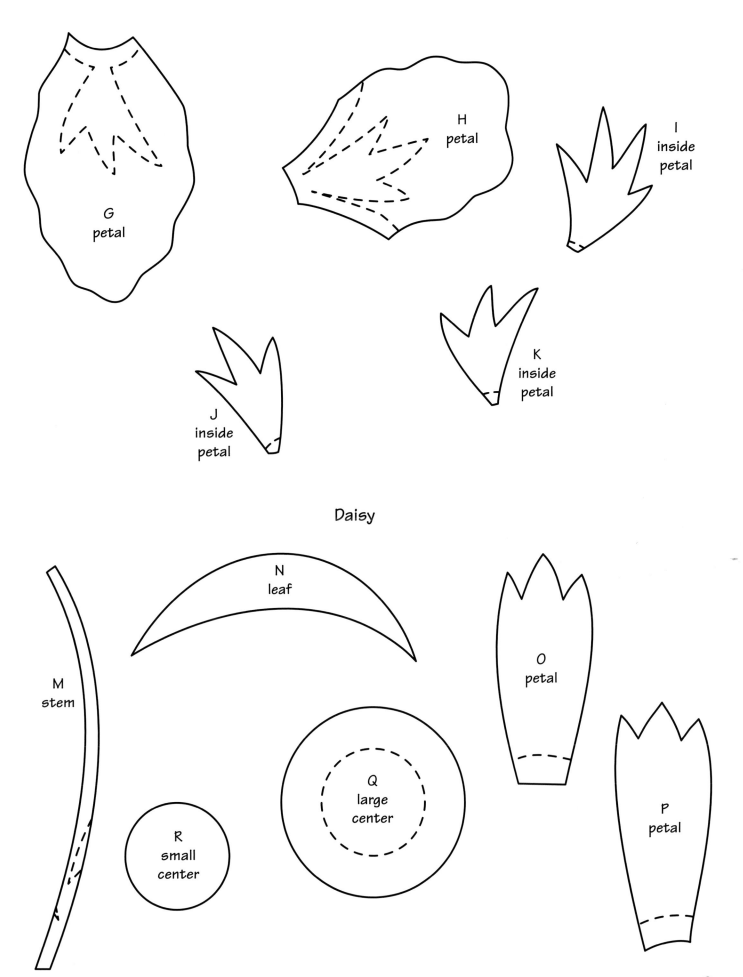

G
petal

H
petal

I
inside
petal

J
inside
petal

K
inside
petal

Daisy

M
stem

N
leaf

O
petal

P
petal

Q
large
center

R
small
center

Primrose

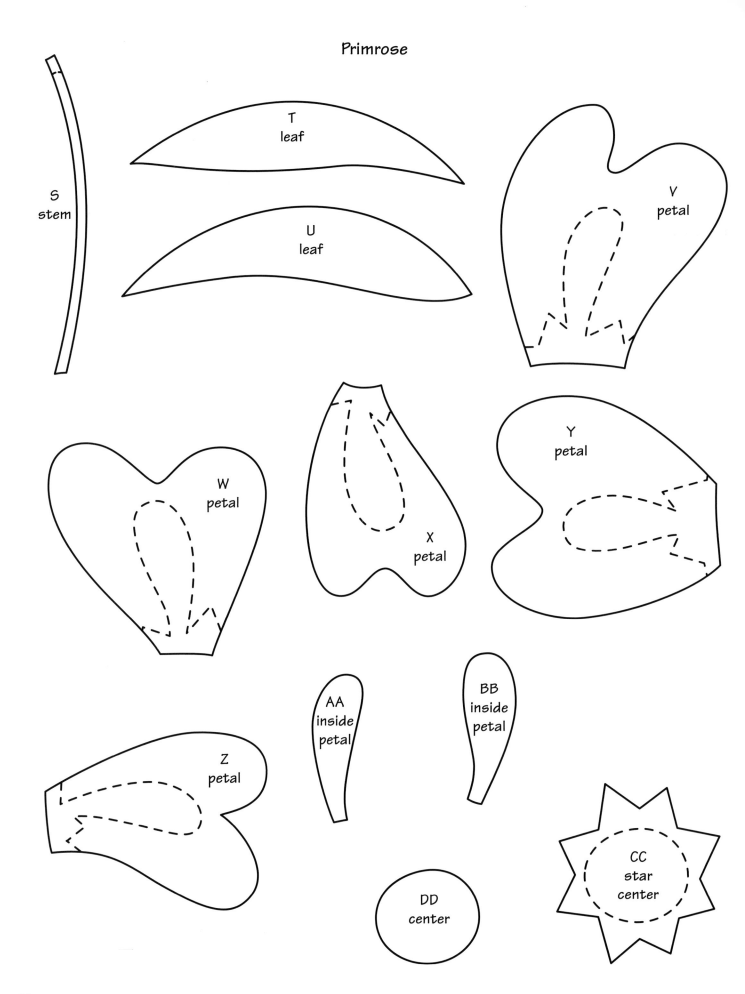

S
stem

T
leaf

U
leaf

V
petal

W
petal

X
petal

Y
petal

Z
petal

AA
inside
petal

BB
inside
petal

DD
center

CC
star
center

10

Poppy

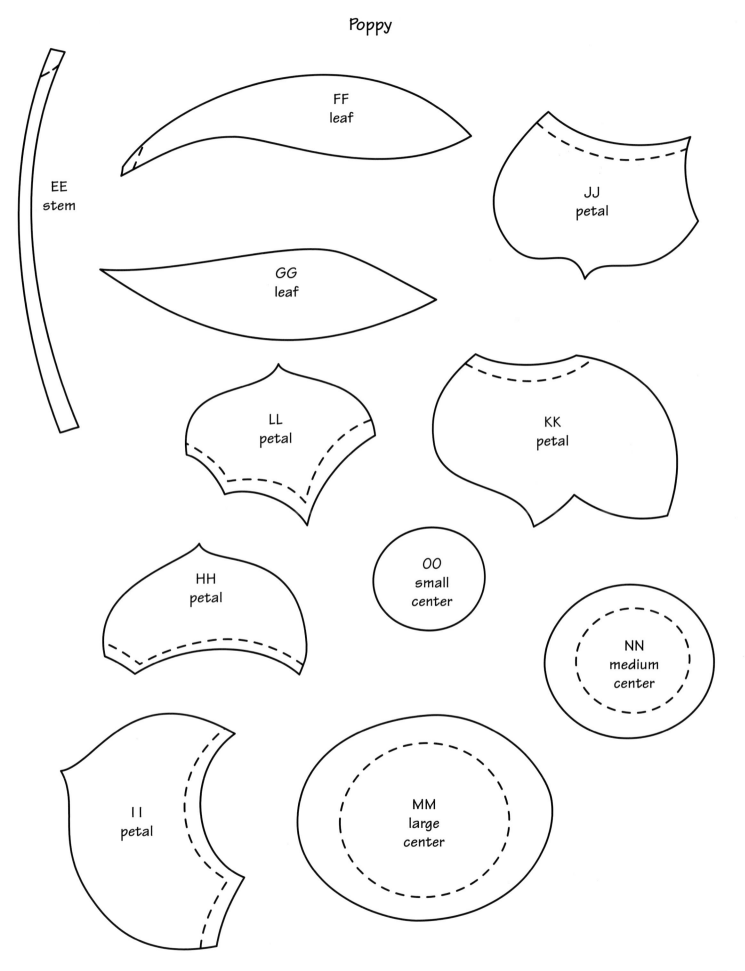

EE
stem

FF
leaf

JJ
petal

GG
leaf

LL
petal

KK
petal

HH
petal

OO
small
center

NN
medium
center

II
petal

MM
large
center

star & pine *wall hanging*

Finished Block Size: 11¼" x 11¼" (29 cm x 29 cm)
Finished Wall Hanging Size: 33½" x 33½" (85 cm x 85 cm)

YARDAGE REQUIREMENTS

Yardage is based on 43"/44" (109/112 cm) wide fabric.

Four 6" (15 cm) squares **each** of 4 assorted white print fabrics for **background squares**

¼ yd (23 cm) of red/white check fabric for block borders

⅜ yd (34 cm) of green stripe fabric for sashing strips and inner border

½ yd (46 cm) of red print fabric for outer borders

1½" x 1½" (4 cm x 4 cm) square of red print fabric for **center square**

1⅛ yds (1 m) of fabric for backing

⅝ yd (57 cm) of fabric for binding

Scraps of assorted brown, red, green, and gold print fabrics for appliqués

You will also need:

38" x 38" (97 cm x 97 cm) piece of batting

Paper-backed fusible web

Stabilizer

CUTTING OUT THE PIECES

*Follow **Rotary Cutting**, page 35, to cut fabric. Squares for backgrounds are cut larger than needed and will be trimmed to correct size after appliquéing. Cutting lengths for borders are exact. You may wish to add an extra 2" to length for "insurance," trimming borders to fit wall hanging top center. All measurements include ¼" seam allowances.*

From red/white check fabric:

- Cut 6 strips 1⅛" wide. From these strips, cut 8 **top/bottom block borders** 1⅛" x 10½" and 8 **side block borders** 1⅛" x 11¾".

From green stripe fabric:

- Cut 6 strips 1½" wide. From these strips, cut 4 **sashing strips** 1½" x 11¾", 2 **top/bottom inner borders** 1½" x 24", and 2 **side inner borders** 1½" x 26".

From red print fabric:

- Cut 2 **top/bottom outer borders** 4" x 26".
- Cut 2 **side outer borders** 4" x 33".

From binding fabric:

- Cut 1 **square** 21" x 21".

CUTTING OUT THE APPLIQUÉS

*Follow **Preparing Fusible Appliqué Pieces**, page 36, to cut appliqués. Appliqué patterns, page 17, do not include seam allowances and are reversed.*

From assorted brown print fabrics:

- Cut 20 **pine stems** (**A**).

From assorted red print fabrics:

- Cut 4 **large stars** (**B**).
- Cut 4 **center berries** (**E**).
- Cut 20 **berries** (**F**).

From assorted green print fabrics:

- Cut 4 **small stars** (**C**).
- Cut 40 **pine needles** ⅛" x 1" (**G**).
- Cut 40 **pine needles** ⅛" x 1⅛" (**H**).
- Cut 40 **pine needles** ⅛" x 1¼" (**I**).

From assorted gold print fabrics:

- Cut 4 **ovals** (**D**).

MAKING THE BLOCKS

*Follow **Machine Piecing** and **Pressing**, page 36, to make the blocks. Use a ¼" seam allowance for all seams.*

1. Sew 4 **background squares** together to make **Background**. Make 4 Backgrounds.

Background (make 4)

2. Center and fuse appliqués in place.
3. Follow **Satin Stitch Appliqué**, page 36, to secure appliqués in place.
4. Centering design, trim background to 10¹/₂" x 10¹/₂".
5. Sew **top/bottom block borders** to **background**. Sew **side block borders** to **background** to make **Block**. Make 4 Blocks.

Block (make 4)

ASSEMBLING THE WALL HANGING

*Refer to **Wall Hanging Diagram** for placement.*
1. Sew 2 **Blocks** and 1 **sashing strip** together to make a **Row**. Make 2 **Rows**.
2. Sew 2 **sashing strips** and 1 **center square** together to make **Sashing Row**.

3. Sew **Rows** and **Sashing Row** together to make **Wall Hanging Top Center**.

ADDING THE BORDERS
1. Matching centers and corners, sew **top/bottom inner borders** to **wall hanging top center**. Sew **side inner borders** to **wall hanging top center**.
2. Matching centers and corners, sew **top/bottom outer borders** to **wall hanging top**. Sew **side outer borders** to **wall hanging top** to complete wall hanging top.

COMPLETING THE WALL HANGING
1. Follow **Quilting**, page 38, to mark, layer, and quilt as desired. Our wall hanging is machine quilted in the ditch around the inner borders and the sashing strips. It is outline quilted around the stars, stems, needles, and berries.
2. Follow **Making A Hanging Sleeve**, page 39, to make and attach a hanging sleeve.
3. Follow **Making A Continuous Bias Strip**, page 40, to prepare 2¹/₂" wide binding.
4. Follow **Attaching Binding With Mitered Corners**, page 41, to attach binding to wall hanging.

Wall Hanging Diagram

star & pine *pillow*

Finished Pillow Size: 17½" x 17½" (44 cm x 44 cm)

YARDAGE REQUIREMENTS

Yardage is based on 43"/44" (109/112 cm) wide fabric.

- 6" x 6" (15 cm x 15 cm) square **each** of 4 white prints
- ⅛ yd (11 cm) of red stripe fabric for inner border
- ⅞ yd (80 cm) of green print fabric for outer border and back
- ½ yd (46 cm) of red solid fabric for welting

⅝ yd (57 cm) of lining fabric

Scraps of assorted brown, red, green, and gold print fabrics for appliqués

You will also need:

- 2⅜ yds (2.2 m) of ¼" (6 mm) diameter cord for welting
- Polyester fiberfill
- Paper-backed fusible web
- Stabilizer

CUTTING OUT THE PIECES

*Follow **Rotary Cutting**, page 35, to cut fabric. Follow **Making A Continuous Bias Strip**, page 40, to cut bias strip. All measurements include ¹/₄" seam allowances.*

From red stripe fabric:
- Cut 2 **inner side borders** 1¹/₄" x 12".
- Cut 2 **inner top/bottom borders** 1¹/₄" x 10¹/₂".

From green print fabric:
- Cut 2 **outer side borders** 3¹/₂" x 18".
- Cut 2 **outer top/bottom borders** 3¹/₂" x 12".
- Cut **pillow back** 18" x 18".

From red solid fabric:
- Cut 1 **bias strip** 2" x 80", pieced as necessary.

From lining fabric:
- Cut 2 **lining squares** 18" x 18".

CUTTING OUT THE APPLIQUÉS

*Follow **Preparing Fusible Appliqué Pieces**, page 36, to cut appliqués. Appliqué patterns, page 17, do not include seam allowances and are reversed.*

From assorted brown print fabrics:
- Cut 5 **pine stems** (A).

From assorted red print fabrics:
- Cut 1 **small star** (C).
- Cut 1 **center berry** (E).
- Cut 5 **berries** (F).

From assorted green print fabrics:
- Cut 1 **large star** (B).
- Cut 10 **pine needles** ¹/₈" x 1" (G).
- Cut 10 **pine needles** ¹/₈" x 1¹/₈" (H).
- Cut 10 **pine needles** ¹/₈" x 1¹/₄" (I).

From assorted gold print fabrics:
- Cut 1 **oval** (D).

MAKING THE PILLOW

*Use a ¹/₄" seam allowance for all seams. Refer to **Pillow Top Diagram** for placement.*

1. Sew 4 white print **squares** together to make **background square**.
2. Center and fuse appliqués to **background square**.
3. Follow **Satin Stitch Appliqué**, page 36, to secure appliqués in place.
4. Centering the design within the square, trim **background square** to 10¹/₂" x 10¹/₂".
5. Matching centers and corners, sew **inner top** and **bottom borders** to **background square**. Sew **inner side borders** to **background square**.
6. Matching centers and corners, sew **outer top** and **bottom borders** to **background square**. Sew **outer side borders** to **background square** to make **pillow front**.
7. Baste a **lining square** to wrong side of **pillow front** and **pillow back**.
8. Follow **Quilting**, page 38, to quilt pillow front as desired. Our pillow front is machine outline quilted around the star.
9. Follow **Pillow Finishing**, page 42, to add welting to pillow top and to finish pillow.

Pillow Top Diagram

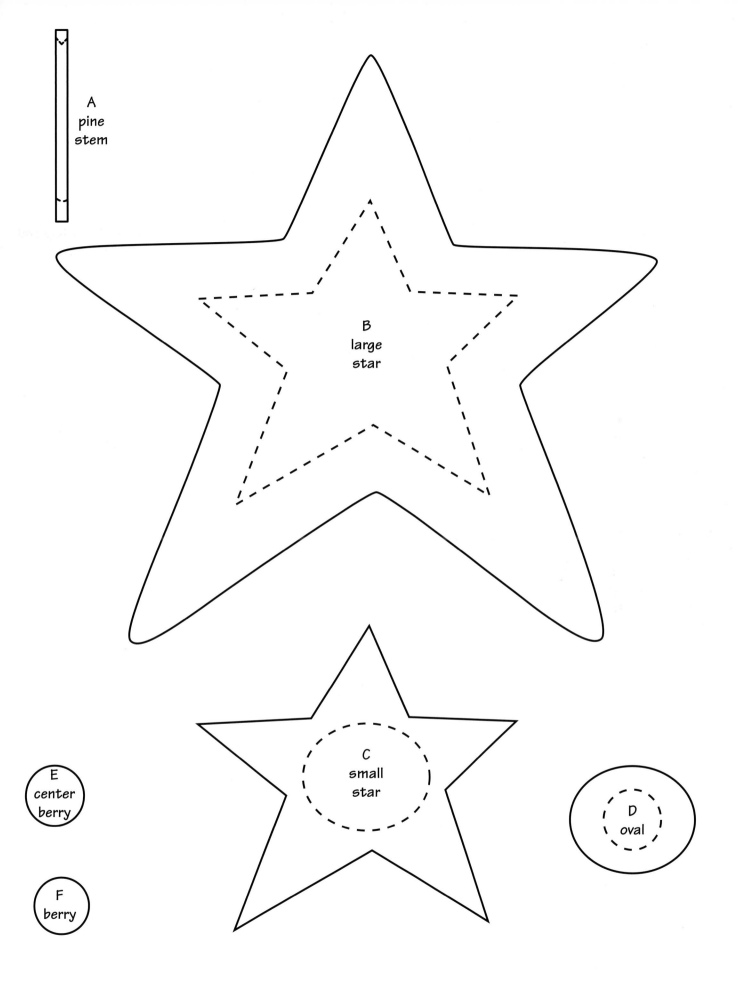

A
pine
stem

B
large
star

C
small
star

E
center
berry

F
berry

D
oval

White Rose & Berry *wall hanging*

Finished Block Size: 11½" x 11½" (29 cm x 29 cm)
Finished Wall Hanging Size: 46" x 46" (117 cm x 117 cm)

YARDAGE REQUIREMENTS

Yardage is based on 43"/44" (109/112 cm) wide fabric.

- ¼ yd (23 cm) **each** of red #1 and cream print fabrics for backgrounds
- ⅜ yd (34 cm) **each** of light green print, dark green print, cream print, and red stripe fabrics for blocks
- ¼ yd (23 cm) of red #2 print fabric for inner borders
- 1½ yds (1.4 m) of green print fabric for outer borders
- 2⅞ yds (2.6 m) of fabric for backing
- ½ yd (46 cm) of fabric for binding
- Scraps of assorted green print, red print, gold print, and white solid fabrics for appliqués

You will also need:

- 50" x 50" (127 cm x 127 cm) piece of batting
- Paper-backed fusible web
- Stabilizer

CUTTING OUT THE PIECES

*Follow **Rotary Cutting**, page 35, to cut fabric. Cutting lengths for borders are exact. You may wish to add an extra 2" to length for "insurance," trimming borders to fit wall hanging top center. All measurements include ¼" seam allowances.*

From red #1 print fabric:
- Cut 1 strip 8" wide. From this strip, cut 5 **background squares** 8" x 8".

From cream print fabric:
- Cut 1 strip 8" wide. From this strip, cut 4 **background squares** 8" x 8".

From light green print fabric:
- Cut 2 **strips** 4½" x 32".

From dark green print fabric:
- Cut 2 **strips** 1¾" x 26".
- Cut 2 **strips** 4¼" x 26".

From cream print fabric:
- Cut 2 **strips** 1¾" x 32".
- Cut 2 **strips** 4¼" x 32".

From red stripe fabric:
- Cut 2 **strips** 4½" x 26".

From red #2 print fabric:
- Cut 2 **top/bottom inner borders** 1¾" x 35".
- Cut 2 **side inner borders** 1¾" x 37½".

From green print fabric:
- Cut 2 **lengthwise side outer borders** 4½" x 45½".
- Cut 2 **lengthwise top/bottom outer borders** 4½" x 37½".

From binding fabric:
- Cut 5 **binding strips** 2½" wide.

CUTTING OUT THE APPLIQUÉS

*Follow **Preparing Fusible Appliqué Pieces**, page 36, to cut appliqués. Appliqué patterns, page 24, do not include seam allowances and are reversed.*

From assorted green print fabrics:
- Cut 2 **stems** (A); cut 2 **stems** (A) in reverse.
- Cut 4 **large berry leaves** (B).
- Cut 12 **small berry leaves** (C).
- Cut 25 **flower leaves** (E).
- Cut 5 **outer flower centers** (G).

From assorted red print fabrics:
- Cut 20 **berries** (D).

From gold print fabric:
- Cut 5 **inner flower centers** (H).

From white solid fabric:
- Cut 25 **flower petals** (F).

MAKING THE BLOCKS

Follow **Machine Piecing** *and* **Pressing**, *page 36, to make the blocks. Use a ¹/₄" seam allowance for all seams. Refer to block photos for placement.*

Berry Block

1. Center and fuse appliqués A-D in place on cream print background squares.
2. Follow **Satin Stitch Appliqué**, page 36, to secure appliqués in place. Trim background squares to 7" x 7".
3. Sew a 1³/₄"w dark green strip to each side of a 4¹/₂"w red stripe strip to make **Strip Set A**. Cut across Strip Set A at 3" intervals to make 8 **Unit 1's**.

Strip Set A   **Unit 1** (make 8)

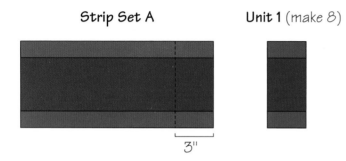

4. Sew a 4¹/₄"w dark green strip to each side of a 4¹/₂"w red stripe strip to make **Strip Set B**. Cut across Strip Set B at 3" intervals to make 8 **Unit 2's**.

Strip Set B   **Unit 2** (make 8)

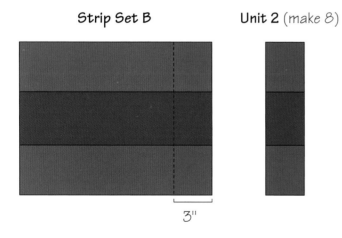

5. Sew **Unit 1's** to each side of the appliquéd background square.

6. Sew **Unit 2's** to remaining sides of the appliquéd background square to make **Berry Block**. Make 4 Berry Blocks.

Berry Block (make 4)

Flower Block

1. Working in alphabetical order, center and fuse appliqués E-H on red print background squares.
2. Follow **Satin Stitch Appliqué**, page 36, to secure appliqués in place.
3. Sew a 1³/₄"w cream print strip to each side of a 4¹/₂"w light green strip to make **Strip Set C**. Cut across Strip Set C at 3" intervals to make 10 **Unit 3's**.

Strip Set C   **Unit 3** (make 10)

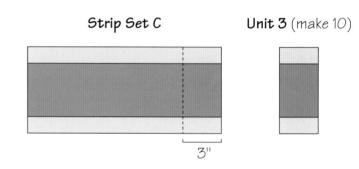

4. Sew a 4¹/₄"w cream print strip to each side of a 4¹/₂"w light green strip to make **Strip Set D**. Cut across Strip Set D at 3" intervals to make 10 **Unit 4's**.

Strip Set D   **Unit 4** (make 10)

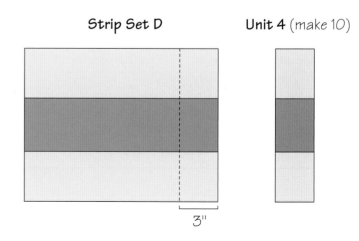

5. Sew **Unit 3's** to each side of the appliquéd background square.
6. Sew **Unit 4's** to remaining sides of the appliquéd background square to make **Flower Block**. Make 5 Flower Blocks.

Flower Block (make 5)

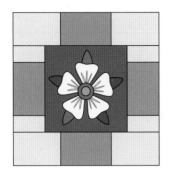

ASSEMBLING THE WALL HANGING

1. Sew 2 **Flower Blocks** and 1 **Berry Block** together to make **Row A**. Make 2 **Row A's**.
2. Sew 2 **Berry Blocks** and 1 **Flower Block** together to make **Row B**.
3. Sew **Row A's** and **Row B** together to make **Wall Hanging Top Center**.

ADDING THE BORDERS

1. Matching centers and corners, sew **top/bottom inner borders** to **wall hanging top center**. Sew **side inner borders** to **wall hanging top center**.
2. Matching centers and corners, sew **top/bottom outer borders** to **wall hanging top**. Sew **side outer borders** to **wall hanging top** to complete wall hanging top.

COMPLETING THE WALL HANGING

1. Follow **Quilting**, page 38, to mark, layer, and quilt as desired. Our wall hanging is machine outline quilted inside the appliquéd squares and around the appliqués. It is quilted in the ditch around each block and appliquéd square and along the inside and outside of the narrow borders. It is outline quilted around the flowers and twice around the sprigs of berries. Detail lines are quilted in the flower petals. There is a decorative quilt design on the borders of each of the blocks and a wavy design on the inner and outer borders.
2. Follow **Making A Hanging Sleeve**, page 39, to make and attach a hanging sleeve if desired.
3. Use binding strips and follow **Making Straight-Grain Binding**, page 40, to prepare binding.
4. Follow **Binding**, page 40, to attach binding to wall hanging.

Berry Block

Flower Block

Berry Table *runner*

Finished Block Size: 11 1/2" x 11 1/2" (29 cm x 29 cm) • **Finished Table Runner Size:** 20" x 44 1/2" (51 cm x 113 cm)

YARDAGE REQUIREMENTS

Yardage is based on 43"/44" (109/112 cm) wide fabric.

- 1/4 yd (23 cm) of cream print fabric for backgrounds
- 1/4 yd (23 cm) **each** of red stripe and dark green print fabric for blocks
- 1/4 yd (23 cm) of red print fabric for inner borders and sashing strips
- 1/2 yd (46 cm) of green print fabric for outer borders
- 1 3/8 yds (1.3 m) of fabric for backing
- Scraps of assorted green print and red print fabrics for appliqués

You will also need:
- 20 1/2" x 45" (52 cm x 114 cm) piece of batting
- Paper-backed fusible web
- Stabilizer

CUTTING OUT THE PIECES

*Follow **Rotary Cutting**, page 35, to cut fabric. All measurements include 1/4" seam allowances.*

From cream print fabric:
- Cut 3 **background squares** 7" x 7".

From red stripe fabric:
- Cut 2 **strips** 4 1/2" x 19".

From dark green print fabric:
- Cut 2 **strips** 1 3/4" x 19".
- Cut 2 **strips** 4 1/4" x 19".

From red print fabric:
- Cut 2 **sashing strips** 1 1/4" x 12".
- Cut 2 **short inner borders** 1 1/4" x 12".
- Cut 2 **long inner borders** 1 1/4" x 38".

From green print fabric:
- Cut 2 **short outer borders** 4" x 13 1/2".
- Cut 2 **long outer borders** 4" x 45", pieced as needed.

From fabric for backing:
- Cut 1 **table runner back** 20 1/2" x 45".

CUTTING OUT THE APPLIQUÉS

*Follow **Preparing Fusible Appliqué Pieces**, page 36, to cut appliqués. Appliqué patterns, page 24, do not include seam allowances and are reversed.*

From assorted green print fabrics:
- Cut 2 **stems** (A); cut 1 **stem** (A) in reverse.
- Cut 3 **large berry leaves** (B).
- Cut 9 **small berry leaves** (C).

From assorted red print fabrics:
- Cut 15 **berries** (D).

ASSEMBLING THE TABLE RUNNER

*Follow **Machine Piecing** and **Pressing**, page 36, to make the blocks. Use a 1/4" seam allowance for all seams. Refer to **Table Runner Diagram**, page 24, for placement.*

Berry Block

1. Follow **Making The Blocks**, Berry Block, page 20, Steps 3-6, to make 6 Unit 1's and 6 Unit 2's. Make 3 Berry Blocks. Do not Satin Stitch appliqués at this time.

Berry Block (make 3)

2. Sew 3 **Berry Blocks** and 2 **sashing strips** together to make **Table Runner Top Center**.

ADDING THE BORDERS

1. Matching centers and corners, sew **short inner borders** to Table Runner Top Center. Sew **long inner borders** to Table Runner Top Center.

2. Matching centers and corners, sew **short outer borders** to Table Runner Top. Sew **long outer borders** to Table Runner Top to complete Table Runner.

COMPLETING THE TABLE RUNNER

1. Layer table runner top and table runner back (right sides facing). Place batting on top. Stitch around table runner, leaving an opening for turning. Turn table runner right side out; sew opening closed.

2. Follow **Satin Stitch Appliqué**, page 36, to secure appliqués in place through all layers.

3. Follow **Quilting**, page 38, to mark, layer, and quilt as desired. Our Table Runner is machine quilted in the ditch around each appliquéd square and in the ditch along each narrow border. It is echo quilted around the appliqués and there is decorative stitching in the block borders.

Table Runner Diagram

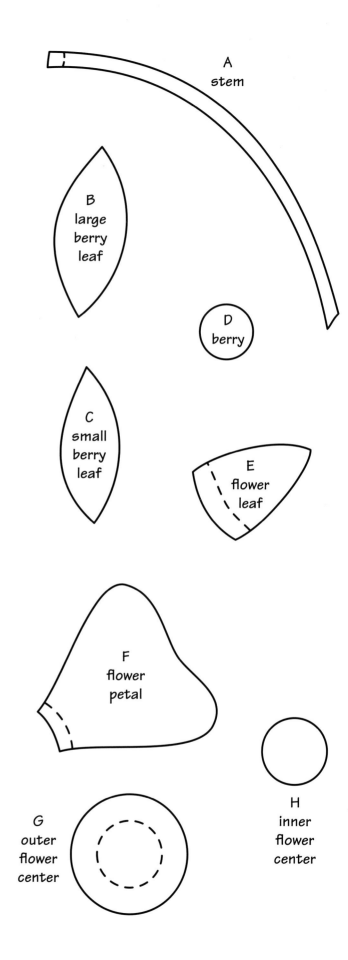

Winterberry & Holly *wall hanging*

Quilt assembled by Rosie Grinstead.

Finished Block Size: 11½" x 11½" (29 cm x 29 cm)

Finished Wall Hanging Size: 35¾" x 35¾" (91 cm x 91 cm)

YARDAGE REQUIREMENTS

Yardage is based on 43"/44" (109/112 cm) wide fabric.

- ³⁄₈ yd (34 cm) **each** of 4 assorted white print fabrics for backgrounds
- ¹⁄₄ yd (23 cm) of light green print fabric for block borders
- ³⁄₈ yd (34 cm) of red print fabric for sashing strips and inner borders
- ⁵⁄₈ yd (57 cm) of green print fabric for outer borders
- 1³⁄₄" x 1³⁄₄" (4 cm x 4 cm) square of green print fabric for **center square**
- 1¹⁄₈ yds (1 m) of fabric for backing
- ³⁄₈ yd (34 cm) of fabric for binding
- Scraps of assorted green and red print fabrics for appliqués

You will also need:
- 40" x 40" (102 cm x 102 cm) piece of batting
- Paper-backed fusible web
- Stabilizer

CUTTING OUT THE PIECES

*Follow **Rotary Cutting**, page 35, to cut fabric. Cutting lengths for borders are exact. You may wish to add an extra 2" for "insurance," trimming borders to fit wall hanging top center. All measurements include ¹⁄₄" seam allowances.*

From each assorted white print fabric:
- Cut 1 **square** 11¹⁄₄" x 11¹⁄₄".

From light green print fabric:
- Cut 8 **top/bottom block borders** 1¹⁄₄" x 12".
- Cut 8 **side block borders** 1¹⁄₄" x 10¹⁄₂".

From red print fabric:
- Cut 4 **sashing strips** 1³⁄₄" x 12".
- Cut 2 **side inner borders** 1³⁄₄" x 24³⁄₄".
- Cut 2 **top/bottom inner borders** 1³⁄₄" x 27¹⁄₄".

From green print fabric:
- Cut 2 **top/bottom outer borders** 4¹⁄₂" x 27¹⁄₄".
- Cut 2 **side outer borders** 4¹⁄₂" x 35¹⁄₄".

From binding fabric:
- Cut 4 **binding strips** 2¹⁄₂" wide.

CUTTING OUT THE APPLIQUÉS

*Follow **Preparing Fusible Appliqué Pieces**, page 36, to cut appliqués. Appliqué patterns, page 29, do not include seam allowances and are reversed.*

From scraps of assorted green print fabrics:
- Cut 16 **stems** (A).
- Cut 16 **large leaves** (B); cut 16 **large leaves** (B) in reverse.
- Cut 16 **small leaves** (C); cut 16 **small leaves** (C) in reverse.
- Cut 16 **whole holly leaves** (D).
- Cut 16 **half holly leaves** (E).

From scraps of assorted red print fabrics:
- Cut 4 **large berries** (F).
- Cut 32 **small berries** (G).

MAKING THE BLOCKS

*Follow **Machine Piecing** and **Pressing**, page 36, to make the blocks. Use a ¹⁄₄" seam allowance for all seams. Refer to block photos, page 29, for placement.*

1. Draw a diagonal line (corner to corner) in both directions on wrong side of 2 **squares**. With right sides together, place 1 marked square on top of 1 unmarked square. Stitch ¹⁄₄" from each side of 1 drawn line (**Fig. 1**).

Fig. 1

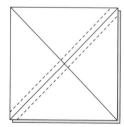

2. Cut along drawn line and press open to make 2 **Triangle-Squares**. Make 4 Triangle-Squares.

Triangle-Square (make 4)

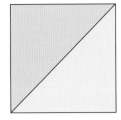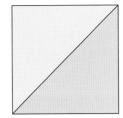

3. On wrong side of 2 Triangle-Squares, extend drawn line from corner of marked triangle to corner of unmarked triangle.
4. Match 1 marked Triangle-Square and 1 unmarked Triangle-Square with matching fabric triangles opposite each other and marked unit on top. Stitch ¼" from each side of drawn line (**Fig. 2**). Cut apart along drawn line to make 2 **Hourglass Blocks**. Open and press seam allowances toward one side. Make 4 Hourglass Blocks.

Fig. 2

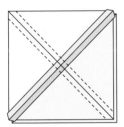

Hourglass Blocks (make 4)

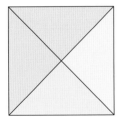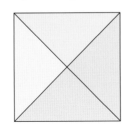

5. Center and fuse appliqués in place on each Hourglass Block.
6. Follow **Satin Stitch Appliqué**, page 36, to secure appliqués in place.
7. Sew **side block borders** to Hourglass Block. Sew **top/bottom block borders** to Hourglass Block to make **Block**. Make 4 Blocks.

Block (make 4)

ASSEMBLING THE WALL HANGING

1. Sew 2 **Blocks** and 1 **sashing strip** together to make a **Row**. Make 2 **Rows**.
2. Sew 2 **sashing strips** and 1 **center square** together to make **Sashing Row**.
3. Sew **Rows** and **Sashing Row** together to make **Wall Hanging Top Center**.

ADDING THE BORDERS

1. Matching centers and corners, sew **side inner borders** to **wall hanging top center**. Sew **top/bottom inner borders** to **wall hanging top center**.
2. Matching centers and corners, sew **top/bottom outer borders** to **wall hanging top**. Sew **side outer borders** to **wall hanging top** to complete wall hanging top.

COMPLETING THE WALL HANGING

1. Follow **Quilting**, page 38, to mark, layer, and quilt as desired. Our wall hanging is machine quilted in the ditch around the inner borders and the sashing strips. It is also echo quilted around the holly, stems, leaves, and berries.

2. Follow **Making A Hanging Sleeve**, page 39, to make and attach a hanging sleeve if desired.

3. Use binding strips and follow **Making Straight-Grain Binding**, page 40, to prepare binding.

4. Follow **Attaching Binding With Mitered Corners**, page 41, to attach binding to wall hanging.

Wall Hanging Diagram

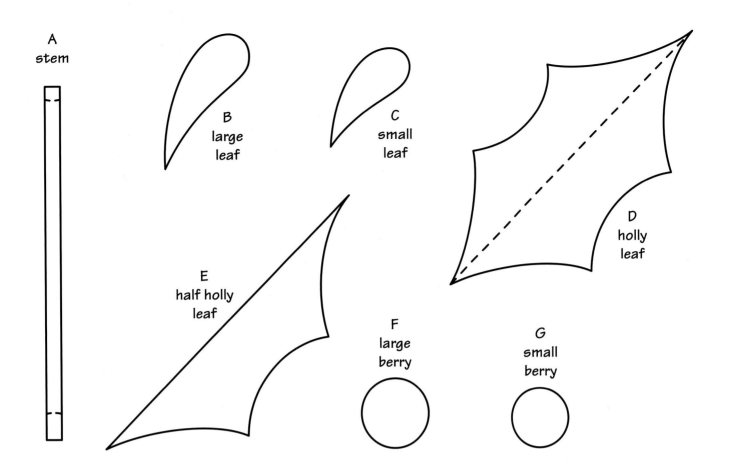

A
stem

B
large
leaf

C
small
leaf

D
holly
leaf

E
half holly
leaf

F
large
berry

G
small
berry

Antiqué Rose *wall hanging*

Wall hanging assembled by Rosie Grinstead and quilted by Jan Zyck.
Finished Block Size: 12" x 12" (30 cm x 30 cm)
Finished Wall Hanging Size: 37" x 37" (94 cm x 94 cm)

YARDAGE REQUIREMENTS

Yardage is based on 43"/44" (109/112 cm) wide fabric.

- 1/4 yd (23 cm) **each** of 2 assorted light cream print fabrics for backgrounds
- 1/2 yd (46 cm) of tan print fabric for block borders
- 1/4 yd (23 cm) of cream print fabric for sashings
- 1/4 yd (23 cm) of medium pink print fabric for inner borders and center square
- 5/8 yd (57 cm) of floral print fabric for outer borders
- 1 1/4 yds (1.1 m) of fabric for backing
- 1/2 yd (46 cm) of fabric for binding
- Scraps of assorted green, light pink, medium pink, dark pink, and light tan print fabrics for appliqués

You will also need:
- 41" x 41" (104 cm x 104 cm) piece of batting
- Paper-backed fusible web
- Stabilizer

CUTTING OUT THE PIECES

*Follow **Rotary Cutting**, page 35, to cut fabric. Cutting lengths for borders are exact. You may wish to add an extra 2" for "insurance," trimming borders to fit wall hanging top center. All measurements include 1/4" seam allowances.*

From each of 2 assorted light cream print fabrics:
- Cut 2 **background squares** 7 1/2" x 7 1/2".

From tan print fabric:
- Cut 5 strips 3"w. From these strips, cut 8 **top/bottom block borders** 3" x 12 1/2" and 8 **side block borders** 3" x 7 1/2".

From cream print fabric:
- Cut 2 strips 2 1/2"w. From these strips, cut 4 **sashing strips** 2 1/2" x 12 1/2".

From medium pink print fabric:
- Cut 1 **center square** 2 1/2" x 2 1/2".
- Cut 2 **top/bottom inner borders** 1 1/2" x 28 1/2".
- Cut 2 **side inner borders** 1 1/2" x 26 1/2".

From floral print fabric:
- Cut 2 **top/bottom outer borders** 4 1/2" x 36 1/2".
- Cut 2 **side outer borders** 4 1/2" x 28 1/2".

From binding fabric:
- Cut 5 **binding strips** 2 1/2" wide.

CUTTING OUT THE APPLIQUÉS

*Follow **Preparing Fusible Appliqué Pieces**, page 36, to cut appliqués. Appliqué patterns, page 33-34, do not include seam allowances and are reversed.*

From scraps of assorted green print fabrics:
- Cut 20 **stems** (A).
- Cut 20 **large leaves** (I).
- Cut 40 **small leaves** (J).

From assorted light pink print fabrics:
- Cut 2 **inner scalloped flowers** (D).
- Cut 2 **inner pointed flowers** (E).

From assorted medium pink print fabrics:
- Cut 2 **outer scalloped flowers** (B).
- Cut 2 **outer pointed flowers** (C).

From assorted dark pink print fabrics:
- Cut 4 **outer flower centers** (F).
- Cut 4 **inner flower centers** (H).
- Cut 20 **berries** (K).

From assorted light tan print fabrics:
- Cut 4 **star centers** (G).

MAKING THE BLOCKS

*Follow **Machine Piecing** and **Pressing**, page 36, to make the blocks. Use a 1/4" seam allowance for all seams. Refer to block photos, page 32, for placement.*

1. Sew **side block borders** to **background square**. Sew **top/bottom block borders** to **background square** to make **Unit 1**. Make 4 Unit 1's.

Unit 1 (make 4)

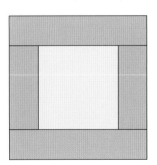

2. Center and fuse appliqués in place on Unit 1.
3. Follow **Satin Stitch Appliqué**, page 36, to secure appliqués in place to make **Flower Block**. Make 4 Flower Blocks.

Flower Block

Flower Block

ASSEMBLING THE WALL HANGING
*Refer to **Wall Hanging Diagram** for placement.*
1. Sew 2 **Flower Blocks** and 1 **sashing strip** together to make **Row**. Make 2 **Rows**.
2. Sew 2 **sashing strips** and 1 **center square** together to make **Sashing Row**.
3. Sew **Rows** and **Sashing Row** together to make **Wall Hanging Top Center**.

ADDING THE BORDERS
1. Matching centers and corners, sew **side inner borders** to **wall hanging top center**. Sew **top/bottom inner borders** to **wall hanging top center**.
2. Matching centers and corners, sew **side outer borders** to **wall hanging top**. Sew **top/bottom outer borders** to **wall hanging top** to complete wall hanging top.

COMPLETING THE WALL HANGING
1. Follow **Quilting**, page 38, to mark, layer, and quilt as desired. Our wall hanging is machine quilted in the ditch around the background square and along each side of the sashing strips and inner borders. There is outline quilting around each appliqué and wavy outline quilting inside each block border. There is a meandering loopy pattern quilted in the inner border and a feather design quilted in the sashing strips and the outer border.
2. Follow **Making A Hanging Sleeve**, page 39, to make and attach a hanging sleeve if desired.
3. Use border strips and follow **Making Straight-Grain Binding**, page 40, to prepare binding.
4. Follow **Attaching Binding With Mitered Corners**, page 41, to attach binding to wall hanging.

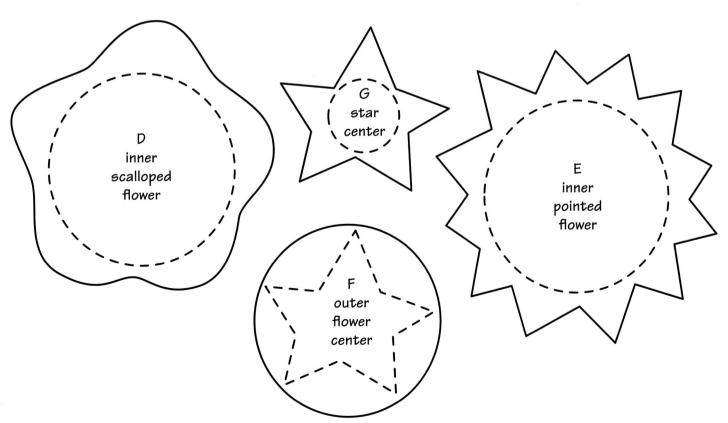

D
inner
scalloped
flower

G
star
center

E
inner
pointed
flower

F
outer
flower
center

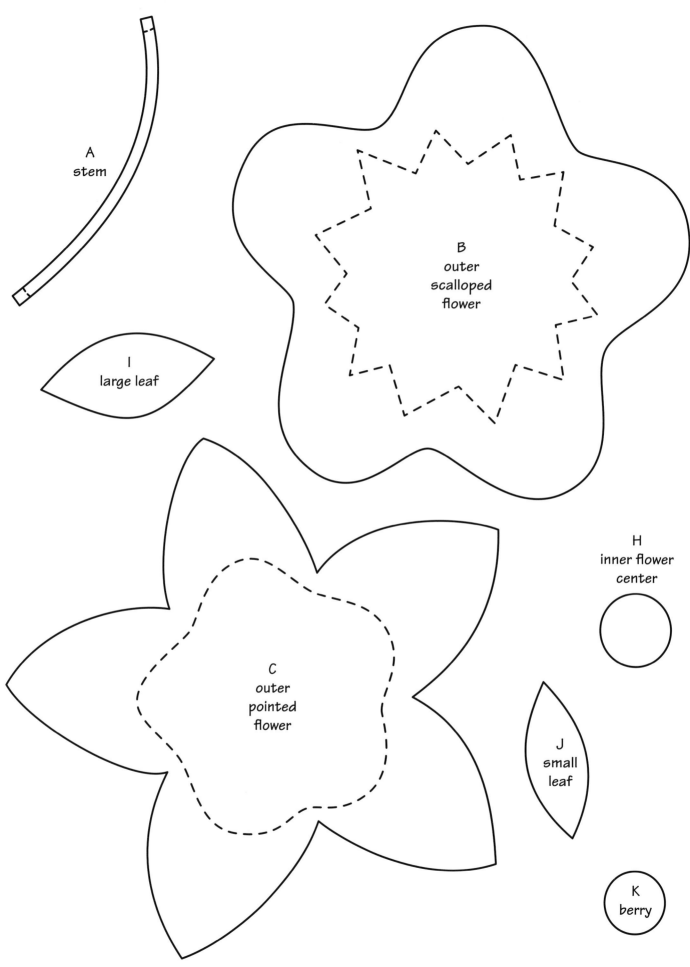

A
stem

B
outer
scalloped
flower

I
large leaf

H
inner flower
center

C
outer
pointed
flower

J
small
leaf

K
berry

General *instructions*

To make your quilting easier and more enjoyable, we encourage you to carefully read all of the general instructions, study the color photographs, and familiarize yourself with the individual project instructions before beginning a project.

FABRICS

SELECTING FABRICS

Choose high-quality, medium-weight 100% cotton fabrics. All-cotton fabrics hold a crease better, fray less, and are easier to quilt than cotton/polyester blends.

Yardage requirements listed for each project are based on 43"/44" wide fabric with a "usable" width of 40" after shrinkage and trimming selvages. Actual usable width will probably vary slightly from fabric to fabric. Our recommended yardage lengths should be adequate for occasional re-squaring of fabric when many cuts are required.

PREPARING FABRICS

We recommend that all fabrics be washed, dried, and pressed before cutting. If fabrics are not pre-washed, washing the finished quilt will cause shrinkage and give it a more "antiqued" look and feel. Bright and dark colors, which may run, should always be washed before cutting. After washing and drying fabric, fold lengthwise with wrong sides together and matching selvages.

ROTARY CUTTING

Rotary cutting has brought speed and accuracy to quiltmaking by allowing quilters to easily cut strips of fabric and then cut those strips into smaller pieces.
- Place fabric on work surface with fold closest to you.

- Cut all strips from the selvage-to-selvage width of the fabric unless otherwise indicated in project instructions.

- Square left edge of fabric using rotary cutter and rulers (**Figs. 1 - 2**).

Fig. 1

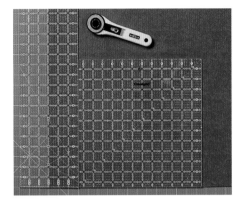

Fig. 2

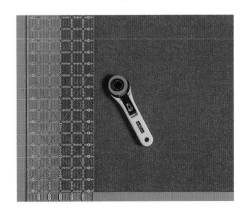

- To cut each strip required for a project, place ruler over cut edge of fabric, aligning desired marking on ruler with cut edge; make cut (**Fig. 3**).

Fig. 3

- When cutting several strips from a single piece of fabric, it is important to make sure that cuts remain at a perfect right angle to the fold; square fabric as needed.

MACHINE PIECING

Precise cutting, followed by accurate piecing, will ensure that all pieces of quilt top fit together well.

- Set sewing machine stitch length for approximately 11 stitches per inch.

- Use neutral-colored general-purpose sewing thread (not quilting thread) in needle and in bobbin.

- An accurate 1/4" seam allowance is **essential**. Presser feet that are 1/4" wide are available for most sewing machines.

- When piecing, always place pieces right sides together and match raw edges; pin if necessary.

- Chain piecing saves time and will usually result in more accurate piecing.

- Trim away points of seam allowances that extend beyond edges of sewn pieces.

SEWING ACROSS SEAM INTERSECTIONS

When sewing across the intersection of two seams, place pieces right sides together and match seams exactly, making sure seam allowances are pressed in opposite directions (**Fig. 4**).

Fig. 4

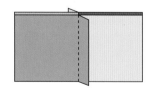

PRESSING

- Use steam iron set on "Cotton" for all pressing.

- Press after sewing each seam.

- Seam allowances are almost always pressed to one side, usually toward darker fabric. However, to reduce bulk it may occasionally be necessary to press seam allowances toward the lighter fabric or even to press them open.

- To prevent dark fabric seam allowance from showing through light fabric, trim darker seam allowance slightly narrower than lighter seam allowance.

- To press long seams, such as those in long strip sets, without curving or other distortion, lay strips across width of the ironing board.

MACHINE APPLIQUÉ
PREPARING FUSIBLE APPLIQUÉ PIECES

White or light-colored fabrics may need to be lined with fusible interfacing before applying fusible web to prevent darker fabrics from showing through.

1. Place paper-backed fusible web, paper side up, over appliqué pattern. Trace pattern onto paper side of web with pencil as many times as indicated in project instructions for a single fabric.
2. Follow manufacturer's instructions to fuse traced patterns to wrong side of fabrics. Do not remove paper backing. (**Note:** Some pieces may be given as measurements, such as 1/8" x 1", instead of drawn patterns. Fuse web to wrong side of the fabrics indicated for these pieces.)
3. Use scissors to cut out appliqué pieces along traced lines; use rotary cutting equipment to cut out appliqué pieces given as measurements. Remove paper backing from all pieces.

SATIN STITCH APPLIQUÉ

A good satin stitch is a smooth line of zigzag stitching that covers the exposed raw edges of appliqué pieces.

1. Pin stabilizer, such as paper or any of the commercially available products, on wrong side of background fabric before stitching appliqués in place.
2. Thread sewing machine with general-purpose thread; use general-purpose thread that matches background fabric in bobbin.

3. Set sewing machine for a narrow zigzag stitch and a medium stitch length. Slightly loosening the top tension may yield a smoother stitch.

4. Begin stitching on appliqués closest to the background and continue to work your way to the appliqué farthest from the background. Begin by stitching two or three stitches in place (drop feed dogs or set stitch length at 0) to anchor thread. Most of the Satin Stitch should be on the appliqué with the right edge of the stitch falling at the outside edge of the appliqué. Stitch over all exposed raw edges of appliqué pieces.

5. (**Note:** Dots on **Figs. 5 – 10** indicate where to leave needle in fabric when pivoting.) For outside corners, stitch just past corner, stopping with needle in background fabric (**Fig. 5**). Raise presser foot. Pivot project, lower presser foot, and stitch adjacent side (**Fig. 6**).

Fig. 5   **Fig. 6**

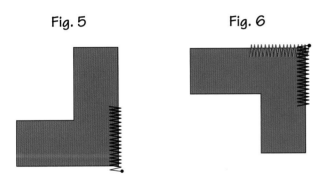

6. For inside corners, stitch just past corner, stopping with needle in appliqué fabric (**Fig. 7**). Raise presser foot. Pivot project, lower presser foot, and stitch adjacent side (**Fig. 8**).

Fig. 7   **Fig. 8**

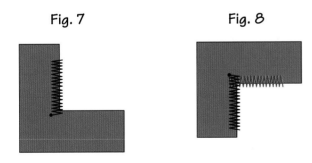

7. When stitching outside curves, stop with needle in background fabric. Raise presser foot and pivot project as needed. Lower presser foot and continue stitching, pivoting as often as necessary to follow curve (**Fig. 9**).

Fig. 9

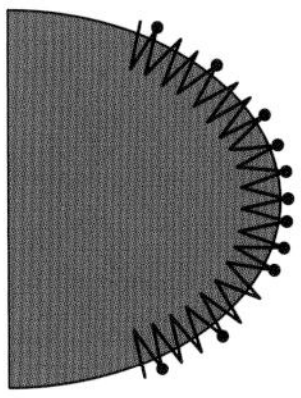

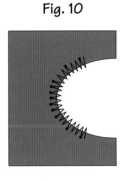

8. When stitching inside curves, stop with needle in appliqué fabric. Raise presser foot and pivot project as needed. Lower presser foot and continue stitching, pivoting as often as necessary to follow curve (**Fig. 10**).

Fig. 10

9. Do not backstitch at end of stitching. Pull threads to wrong side of background fabric; knot thread and trim ends.

10. Carefully tear away stabilizer.

QUILTING

Quilting holds the three layers (top, batting, and backing) of the quilt together and can be done by hand or machine. Because marking, layering, and quilting are interrelated and may be done in different orders depending on circumstances, please read entire **Quilting** section, pages 38-39, before beginning project.

TYPES OF QUILTING DESIGNS

In the Ditch Quilting

Quilting along seamlines or along edges of appliquéd pieces is called "in the ditch" quilting. This type of quilting should be done on side **opposite** seam allowance and does not have to be marked.

Outline Quilting

Quilting a consistent distance, usually ¼", from seam or appliqué is called "outline" quilting. Outline quilting may be marked, or ¼" masking tape may be placed along seamlines for quilting guide. (Do not leave tape on quilt longer than necessary, since it may leave an adhesive residue.)

Motif Quilting

Quilting a design, such as a feathered wreath, is called "motif" quilting. This type of quilting should be marked before basting quilt layers together.

Echo Quilting

Quilting that follows the outline of an appliquéd or pieced design with two or more parallel lines is called "echo" quilting. This type of quilting does not need to be marked.

Crosshatch Quilting

Quilting straight lines in a grid pattern is called "crosshatch" quilting. Lines may be stitched parallel to edges of quilt or stitched diagonally. This type of quilting may be marked or stitched using a guide.

MARKING QUILTING LINES

Quilting lines may be marked using fabric marking pencils, chalk markers, water- or air-soluble pens, or lead pencils.

Simple quilting designs may be marked with chalk or chalk pencil after basting. A small area may be marked, then quilted, before moving to next area to be marked. Intricate designs should be marked before basting using a more durable marker.

Caution: Pressing may permanently set some marks. **Test** different markers **on scrap fabric** to find one that marks clearly and can be thoroughly removed.

A wide variety of pre-cut quilting stencils, as well as entire books of quilting patterns, are available. Using a stencil makes it easier to mark intricate or repetitive designs.

To make a stencil from a pattern, center template plastic over pattern and use a permanent marker to trace pattern onto plastic. Use a craft knife with single or double blade to cut channels along traced lines (**Fig. 11**).

Fig. 11

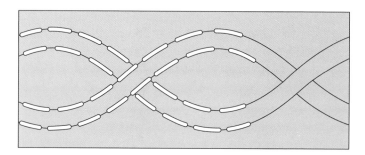

PREPARING THE BACKING

Yardage requirements listed for wall hanging backings are calculated for 43"/44"w fabric.

1. To allow for slight shifting of wall hanging top during quilting, backing should be approximately 2" larger on all sides.
2. Measure length and width of wall hanging top; add 4" to each measurement. Cut a piece of backing fabric the determined measurements.

CHOOSING THE BATTING

The appropriate batting will make quilting easier. For fine hand quilting, choose low-loft batting. All cotton or cotton/polyester blend battings work well for machine quilting because the cotton helps "grip" quilt layers. If quilt is to be tied, a high-loft batting, sometimes called extra-loft or fat batting, may be used to make quilt "fluffy."

Types of batting include cotton, polyester, wool, cotton/polyester blend, cotton/wool blend, and silk.

When selecting batting, refer to package labels for characteristics and care instructions. Cut batting same size as prepared backing.

ASSEMBLING THE QUILT

1. Examine wrong side of quilt top closely; trim any seam allowances and clip any threads that may show through front of the quilt. Press quilt top, being careful not to "set" any marked quilting lines.

2. Place backing **wrong** side up on flat surface. Use masking tape to tape edges of backing to surface. Place batting on top of backing fabric. Smooth batting gently, being careful not to stretch or tear. Center quilt top **right** side up on batting.

3. Use 1" rustproof safety pins to "pin-baste" all layers together, spacing pins approximately 4" apart (**Fig. 12**). Begin at center and work toward outer edges to secure all layers. If possible, place pins away from areas that will be quilted, although pins may be removed as needed when quilting.

Fig. 12

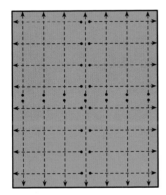

MACHINE QUILTING METHODS

Use general-purpose thread in bobbin. Do not use quilting thread. Thread the needle of machine with general-purpose thread or transparent monofilament thread to make quilting blend with quilt top fabrics. Use decorative thread, such as a metallic or contrasting-color general-purpose thread, to make quilting lines stand out more.

Straight-Line Quilting

The term "straight-line" is somewhat deceptive, since curves (especially gentle ones) as well as straight lines can be stitched with this technique.

1. Set stitch length for six to ten stitches per inch and attach walking foot to sewing machine.

2. Determine which section of quilt will have longest continuous quilting line, oftentimes the area from center top to center bottom. Roll up and secure each edge of quilt to help reduce the bulk, keeping fabrics smooth. Smaller projects may not need to be rolled.

3. Begin stitching on longest quilting line, using very short stitches for the first 1/4" to "lock" quilting. Stitch across project, using one hand on each side of walking foot to slightly spread fabric and to guide fabric through machine. Lock stitches at end of quilting line.

4. Continue machine quilting, stitching longer quilting lines first to stabilize quilt before moving on to other areas.

MAKING A HANGING SLEEVE

Attaching a hanging sleeve to the back of a wall hanging or quilt before the binding is added allows the project to be displayed on a wall.

1. Measure width of quilt top edge and subtract 1". Cut piece of fabric 7" wide by determined measurement.

2. Press short edges of fabric piece 1/4" to wrong side; press edges 1/4" to wrong side again and machine stitch in place.

3. Matching wrong sides, fold piece in half lengthwise to form tube.

4. Follow project instructions to sew binding to quilt top and to trim backing and batting. Before blindstitching binding to backing, match raw edges and stitch hanging sleeve to center top edge on back of quilt.

5. Finish binding quilt, treating hanging sleeve as part of backing.

6. Blindstitch bottom of hanging sleeve to backing, taking care not to stitch through to front of quilt.

MAKING A CONTINUOUS BIAS STRIP

Bias strips can simply be cut and pieced to desired length. However, when a long length of binding is needed, the "continuous" method is quick and accurate.

1. Cut square from binding fabric the size indicated in project instructions. Cut square in half diagonally to make two triangles.

2. With right sides together and using ¼" seam allowance, sew triangles together (**Fig. 13**); press seam allowances open.

Fig. 13

3. On wrong side of fabric, draw lines the width of binding as specified in project instructions (**Fig. 14**). Cut off any remaining fabric less than this width.

Fig. 14

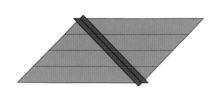

4. With right sides inside, bring short edges together to form tube; match raw edges so that first drawn line of top section meets second drawn line of bottom section (**Fig. 15**).

Fig. 15

5. Carefully pin edges together by inserting pins through drawn lines at point where drawn lines intersect, making sure pins go through intersections on both sides. Using ¼" seam allowance, sew edges together; press seam allowances open.

6. To cut continuous strip, begin cutting along first drawn line (**Fig. 16**). Continue cutting along drawn line around tube.

Fig. 16

7. Trim ends of bias strip square.

8. Matching wrong sides and raw edges, carefully press bias strip in half lengthwise to complete binding.

BINDING

Binding encloses the raw edges of the quilt. Because of its stretchiness, bias binding works well for binding projects with curves or rounded corners and tends to lie smooth and flat in any given circumstance. Binding may also be cut from straight lengthwise or crosswise grain of fabric.

MAKING STRAIGHT-GRAIN BINDING

1. Using diagonal seams, sew binding strips together end to end (**Fig. 17**) to make 1 continuous binding strip.

Fig. 17

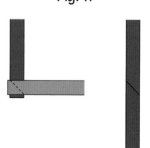

2. Matching wrong sides and raw edges, press strip in half lengthwise to complete binding.

ATTACHING BINDING WITH MITERED CORNERS

1. Beginning with one end near center on bottom edge of quilt, lay binding around quilt to make sure that seams in binding will not end up at a corner. Adjust placement if necessary. Matching raw edges of binding to raw edge of quilt top, pin binding to right side of quilt along one edge.

2. When you reach first corner, mark ¼" from corner of quilt top (**Fig. 18**).

Fig. 18

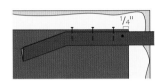

3. Beginning 10" from end of binding and using ¼" seam allowance, sew binding to quilt, backstitching at beginning of stitching and at mark (**Fig. 19**). Lift needle out of fabric and clip thread.

Fig. 19

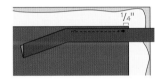

4. Fold binding as shown in **Figs. 20 – 21** and pin binding to adjacent side, matching raw edges. When reaching the next corner, mark ¼" from edge of quilt top.

Fig. 20   Fig. 21

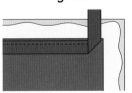 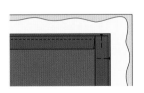

5. Backstitching at edge of quilt top, sew pinned binding to quilt (**Fig. 22**); backstitch at the next mark. Lift needle out of fabric and clip thread.

Fig. 22

6. Continue sewing binding to quilt, stopping approximately 10" from starting point (**Fig. 23**).

Fig. 23

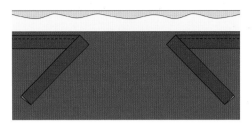

7. Bring beginning and end of binding to center of opening and fold each end back, leaving a ¼" space between folds (**Fig. 24**). Finger-press folds.

Fig. 24

8. Unfold ends of binding and draw a line across wrong side in finger-pressed crease. Draw a line through the lengthwise pressed fold of binding at same spot to create a cross mark. With edge of ruler at marked cross, line up 45° angle marking on ruler with one long side of binding. Draw a diagonal line from edge to edge. Repeat on remaining end, making sure that the two lines are angled the same way (**Fig. 25**).

Fig. 25

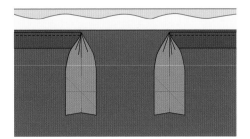

9. Matching right sides and diagonal lines, pin binding ends together at right angles (**Fig. 26**).

Fig. 26

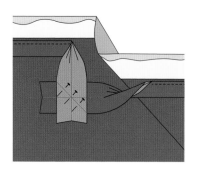

10. Machine stitch along diagonal line, removing pins as you stitch (**Fig. 27**).

Fig. 27

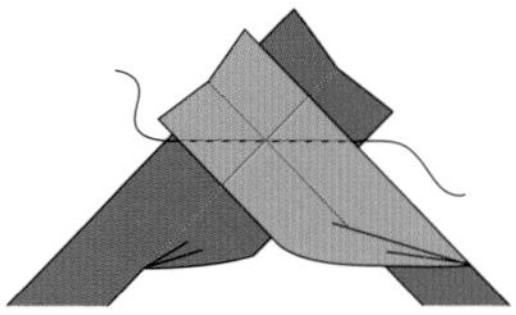

11. Lay binding against quilt to double-check that it is correct length.
12. Trim binding ends, leaving ¼" seam allowance; press seam open. Stitch binding to quilt.
13. Trim backing and batting a scant ¼" larger than quilt top so that batting and backing will fill the binding when it is folded over to quilt backing.
14. On 1 edge of quilt, fold binding over to quilt backing and pin pressed edge in place, covering stitching line (**Fig. 28**). On adjacent side, fold binding over, forming a mitered corner (**Fig. 29**). Repeat to pin remainder of binding in place.

Fig. 28   **Fig. 29**

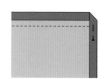

15. Blindstitch (page 43) binding to backing, taking care not to stitch through to front of quilt.

PILLOW FINISHING

1. To make rounded corners, fold pillow back in half twice. Place a round object such as a glass on pillow back corner as shown in **Fig. 30**. Draw around object; trim corners along drawn line. Using the back as a pattern, trim pillow top corners.

Fig. 30

2. To make welting, lay cord along center of bias strip on wrong side of fabric; fold strip over cord. Using a zipper foot, machine baste close to cord. Trim seam allowance to ¼".
3. Matching raw edges and beginning and ending 3" from ends of welting, baste welting to right side of pillow top. To make turning corners easier, clip seam allowance of welting at pillow top corners.
4. Remove approximately 3" of seam at one end of welting; fold fabric away from cord. Trim remaining end of welting so that cord ends meet exactly (**Fig. 31**).

Fig. 31

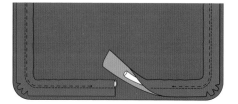

5. Fold short edge of welting fabric ½" to wrong side; fold fabric back over area where ends meet (**Fig. 32**).

Fig. 32

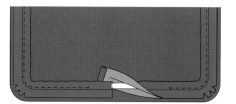

6. Baste remainder of welting to pillow top close to cord (**Fig. 33**).

Fig. 33

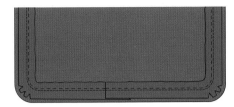

7. Place pillow back and pillow top right sides together. Using a ¼" seam allowance (or stitching as close as possible to the welting), sew pillow top and back together, leaving an opening at bottom edge for turning.

8. Turn pillow right side out, carefully pushing corners outward. Stuff with fiberfill and blindstitch opening closed.

BLIND STITCH
Come up at 1, go down at 2, and come up at 3 (**Fig. 34**). Length of stitches may be varied as desired.

Fig. 34

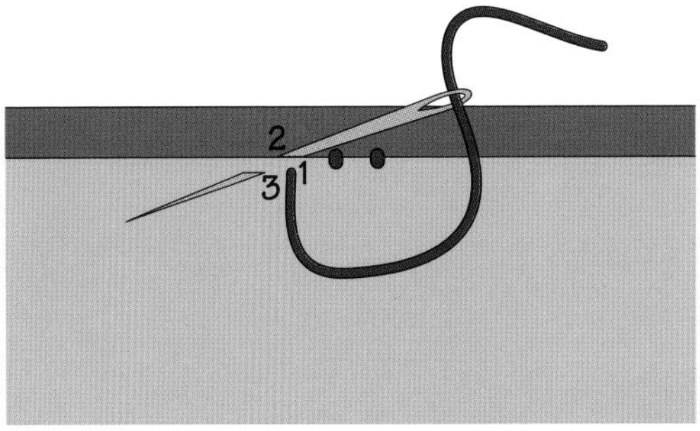

SIGNING AND DATING YOUR QUILT

A completed quilt is a work of art and should be signed and dated. There are many different ways to do this and numerous books on the subject. The label should reflect the style of the quilt, the occasion or person for which it was made, and the quilter's own particular talents. Following are suggestions for recording the history of the quilt or adding a sentiment for future generations.

- *Embroider quilter's name, date, and any additional information on quilt top or backing. Matching floss, such as cream floss on a white background, will leave a subtle record. Bright or contrasting floss will make the information stand out.*

- *Make label from muslin and use permanent marker to write information. Use different colored permanent markers to make label more decorative. Stitch label to back of quilt.*

- *Use photo-transfer paper to add image to white or cream fabric label. Stitch label to back of quilt.*

- *Write message on appliquéd design from quilt top. Attach appliqué to back of the quilt.*

Discover the creative world of Leisure Arts publications, where inspiration lives on every page.

Enjoy more of *jan kornfeind's* heirloom-quality designs!

Leaflet #3827

Leaflet #3930

Your next great idea starts here.